First Facts®

The Middle Ages

Medieval Castles

by Jim Whiting

Consultant:
James Masschaele
Associate Professor of Medieval History
Rutgers University
New Brunswick, New Jersey

Capstone
press®

Mankato, Minnesota

First Facts is published by Capstone Press,
151 Good Counsel Drive, P.O. Box 669, Mankato, Minnesota 56002.
www.capstonepress.com

Library of Congress Cataloging-in-Publication Data
Whiting, Jim, 1951–
    Medieval castles / by Jim Whiting.
    p. cm. — (First facts. The Middle Ages)
    Includes bibliographical references and index.
    Summary: "Describes medieval castles, including why and how they were
built" — Provided by publisher.
    ISBN-13: 978-1-4296-2267-7 (hardcover)
    ISBN-10: 1-4296-2267-9 (hardcover)
    1. Castles — Juvenile literature. 2. Civilization, Medieval — Juvenile literature.
I. Title.
GT3550.W484 2009
940.1 — dc22   2008027078

Editorial Credits

Megan Schoeneberger, editor; Kim Brown, designer; Marcie Spence, photo researcher

Photo Credits

Alamy/Joshua Atticks, 18; Capstone Press/Kim Brown, 5, 21; Corbis/Bettmann, 15 (right);
Getty Images Inc./Popperfoto, 13; The Granger Collection, New York, 7, 8; iStockphoto
/Stefan Ondrejovic, 11; James P. Rowan, 4; Marco ILLESCAS (www.flickr.com/photos/
marcoie), cover; Mary Evans Picture Library, 15 (left); North Wind Picture Archives, 6–7;
Shutterstock/Bill McKelvie, 20; Shutterstock/Demid, 19; Shutterstock/Kris Vandereycken,
1; Shutterstock/TTphoto, 16

**Essential content terms are bold and are defined at the bottom of the page
    where they first appear.**

1 2 3 4 5 6 14 13 12 11 10 09

Table of Contents

Home Sweet Castle?

Would it be fun to live in a castle? Maybe today, but not in the Middle Ages. Castles were cold, dark, and damp. Fireplaces and candles provided the only heat and light. The castle's owner was pretty comfortable. But servants and soldiers shivered under thin blankets on straw mattresses.

Vufflen Castle
Switzerland

Castles of the Middle Ages

Europe
476 – 1500

Urquhart

Beaumaris

Pembroke

Tower of London

Gravensteen

Chillon

Loire River

Brissac

Loches

Eltz

Obidos

Segovia

Castle del Monte

Why Castles Were Built

Kings and queens weren't the only ones living in castles. In Europe, **lords** and other noblemen controlled large areas of land. These men often fought over land. They built castles for protection from attacks.

lord — a man of high rank who has power over other people

Medieval Fact!
Towns often grew around castles. Townspeople came inside castles in times of danger.

Not-So-Fine Dining

In a castle, everyone ate in the great hall. They used spoons, knives, and their fingers. The lord and his family ate off plates. Everyone else ate off thick slices of stale bread called trenchers. The bread soaked up food juices and grease.

Years of Hard Work

Castles took about 10 years to build. Hundreds of men worked on one castle. Oxen dragged huge stone blocks to the site. Men shaped the blocks with hammers and chisels. The stones had to fit tightly together. Workers used pulleys and ropes to lift the blocks into place.

Medieval Fact!

Castles weren't always made of stone. Early castles were made of wood and dirt. But wooden castles burned too easily.

Castle Defenses

Castles were rock solid, but they still needed protection. A wide water-filled ditch called a moat surrounded most castles. A movable drawbridge crossed the moat. The drawbridge was raised in times of danger. The wooden gates had heavy iron grates to keep out attackers.

iron grates

Attack!

During battles, some attackers tried to beat down castle gates. Others climbed ladders up castle walls. Attackers also dug tunnels under castle walls. They hoped the tunnels would cause the walls to fall.

Attackers often used weapons called **catapults**. They hurled stones at castle walls. Catapults also tossed disgusting things like dead animals into castles.

catapult — a weapon with an arm that was pulled back and then released to throw large objects over walls

Defending Their Turf

Castle defenders fought back against attackers. They fired arrows. They also dumped boiling oil or water on enemies. Walkways let them hurry around the tops of castle walls. They ducked behind stone blocks to stay safe. Corner towers let them pick off attackers from different angles.

Under Siege

Sometimes attackers would begin a **siege**. They surrounded the castle and cut off supplies. They hoped the people inside would give up or starve. To prepare for sieges, castle storerooms were jam-packed with food. Castles also had deep wells of fresh water.

siege — the surrounding of a castle or city to cut off supplies

Urquhart Castle

Scotland

The End of Castles

Gunpowder was brought to Europe in the 1300s. Attackers didn't need to climb castle walls anymore. Instead, they set up cannons a safe distance away. The cannons blasted holes in castle walls. Then the attackers would rush into the castle. Castles were no longer the safest place during a battle.

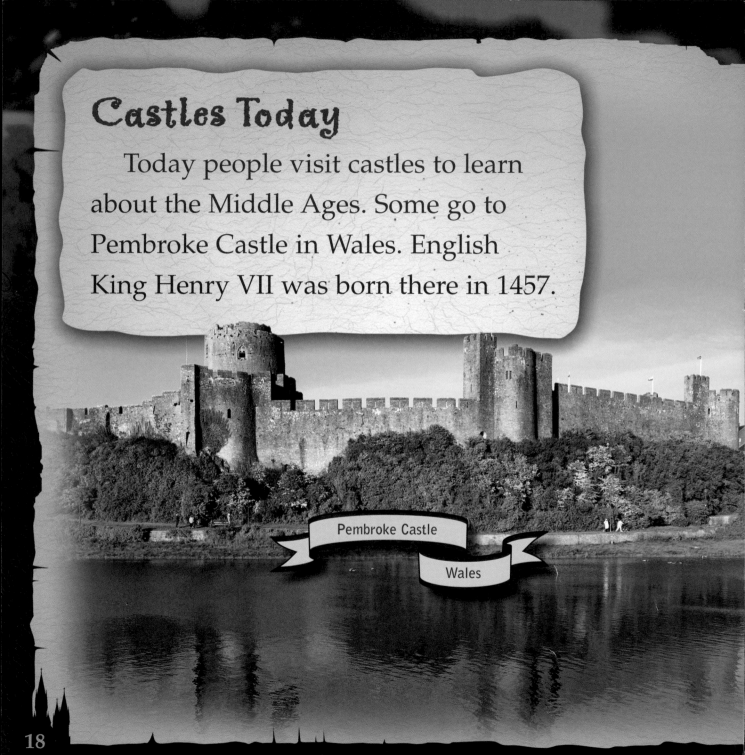

Castles Today

Today people visit castles to learn about the Middle Ages. Some go to Pembroke Castle in Wales. English King Henry VII was born there in 1457.

Pembroke Castle

Wales

Another popular site is the Loire Valley in France. This area boasts hundreds of castles. People can even spend the night in some of them.

Chenonceau Castle

Loire Valley, France

Amazing but True!

Did castles have toilets? Sort of. Toilets were wood or stone slabs with round holes. The waste fell into pits far below.

Workers cleaned these pits. Sometimes, the workers found extra treasure. Coins or jewelry would fall into the pit. Workers dug through the waste with their hands to find them. Finders keepers!

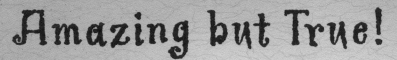

medieval toilet

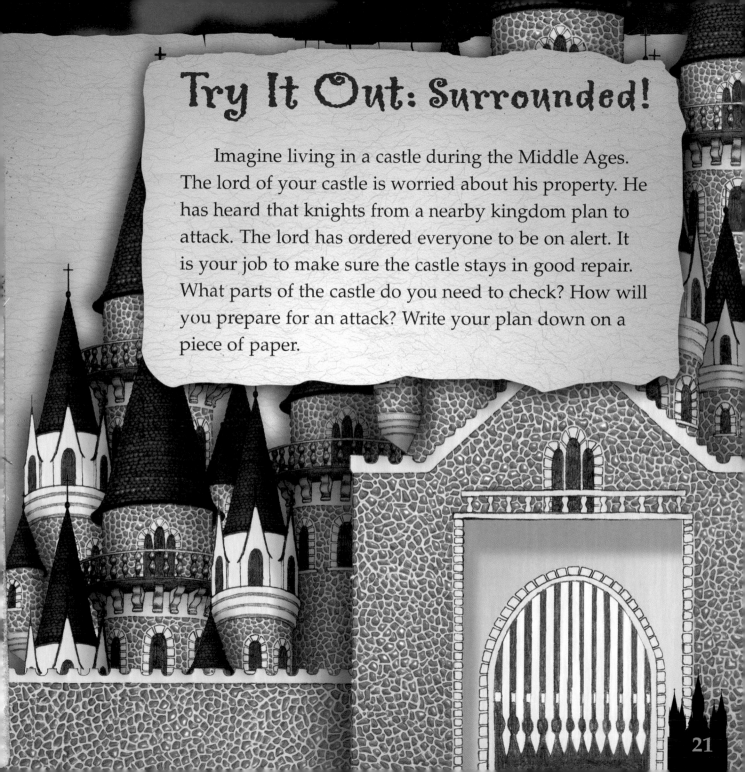

Try It Out: Surrounded!

Imagine living in a castle during the Middle Ages. The lord of your castle is worried about his property. He has heard that knights from a nearby kingdom plan to attack. The lord has ordered everyone to be on alert. It is your job to make sure the castle stays in good repair. What parts of the castle do you need to check? How will you prepare for an attack? Write your plan down on a piece of paper.

Glossary

catapult (KAT-uh-puhlt) — a large weapon, similar to a slingshot, used in the past for firing objects over castle walls

chisel (CHIZ-uhl) — a tool with a flat, sharp end used to cut stone or wood

lord (LORD) — a person of high rank who has great power over other people

moat (MOHT) — a deep, wide ditch dug all around a castle or fort and filled with water to prevent attacks

siege (SEEJ) — the surrounding of a castle or city to cut off supplies and then waiting for those inside to give up

Read More

Adams, Brian. *Medieval Castles.* Hallmarks of History. Mankato, Minn.: Stargazer Books, 2007.

Bruce, Julia. *Siege! Can You Capture a Castle?* Step into History. Berkeley Heights, N.J.: Enslow, 2008.

Coombs, Rachel. *A Year in a Castle.* Time Goes By. Minneapolis: Millbrook Press, 2009.

Shuter, Jane. *The Middle Ages.* History Opens Windows. Chicago: Heinemann, 2007.

Internet Sites

FactHound offers a safe, fun way to find educator-approved Internet sites related to this book.

Here's what you do:
1. Visit *www.facthound.com*
2. Choose your grade level.
3. Begin your search.

This book's ID number is 9781429622677.

FactHound will fetch the best sites for you!

Index